T0118507

LOST AT SEA,
SORT OF

LOST AT SEA, SORT OF

John Taylor Mulder

authorHOUSE®

AuthorHouse™
1663 Liberty Drive
Bloomington, IN 47403
www.authorhouse.com
Phone: 1-800-839-8640

© *2013 by John Taylor Mulder. All rights reserved.*

No part of this book may be reproduced, stored in a retrieval system, or transmitted by any means without the written permission of the author.

Published by AuthorHouse   12/26/2012

ISBN: 978-1-4772-9513-7 (sc)
ISBN: 978-1-4772-9512-0 (e)

Library of Congress Control Number: 2012922725

Any people depicted in stock imagery provided by Thinkstock are models, and such images are being used for illustrative purposes only.
Certain stock imagery © Thinkstock.

This book is printed on acid-free paper.

Because of the dynamic nature of the Internet, any web addresses or links contained in this book may have changed since publication and may no longer be valid. The views expressed in this work are solely those of the author and do not necessarily reflect the views of the publisher, and the publisher hereby disclaims any responsibility for them.

DEDICATION

This book is dedicated to my children, Ashly and Alexander. Just being their dad fills my heart.

PROLOGUE

This book is about choices, focus, survival and how our American based cultural belief systems sometimes "shortcut" our decision making processes. We all have belief systems. They are neither good nor bad. It is the additional information we choose to either include or not include in our decisions that determine the outcome. Our belief system is not limited to religious or spiritual aspects, but include every decision we make about every task we do on a daily basis. What foods we eat, what we watch, read, listen, our friends, our employers; it is an endless list. Without additional information, everything we believe in will produce an expected, less desirable outcome. With additional information, we will make better decisions with a more predictable, desirable outcome.

In this book I share some of my experiences and how I struggled to understand the importance of how to effectively use information. For me, it is the person Jack Mulder that goes overboard at night in the Pacific Ocean and transforms into the person, "Captain Jack". Just a "moment" passes from the time I leave the sailboat until I hit the water. It was that "moment" of understanding along with my beliefs that would determine the outcome.

CHAPTER 1

I am on a 32 foot sailboat in the Pacific Ocean approximately 3 days out of Lahaina, Maui. It is close to midnight, a storm is brewing, the seas are building to 20 foot swells and it has begun to rain. I am sound asleep (actually lightly asleep at sea) and my wife wakes me up after hearing the wind increase in intensity. I could hear our other crewmember calling for my wife and I to get up on deck. Normally I would take time to put on my floatation coveralls before responding. Not tonight because the wind is howling and I knew if we didn't get the main sail reefed (reduced in size) the mast would break or something else terrible would happen. All three crew have been lucky so far. We have been at sea for 24 days and have endured several storms interrupted by absolutely calm, flat windless seas. As I climb the ladder topside I am wearing only a dark short sleeve T-shirt and a pair of black sweatpants. My wife follows me up the ladder to help. My first thought is "why didn't our other crewmember call for help sooner, but then I remember as I try to focus from my slumber that the sea can and does change in an instant. I take a position at the aft end of the boom, the horizontal support that attaches to the mast.

We are trying to turn into the wind in an effort to take the pressure off the main sail so that I can latch the end of the boom with a support cable. That way we can reduce the size of the main sail. The winds continue to increase in velocity, the boat is rising and falling and we are hanging on for dear life. When I reach out to try and secure the boom, the block and tackle that attaches the boom to the deck and also controls the horizontal movement of the boom swing in either direction, …. breaks…. The boom and I swing hard to starboard (to the right facing forward) and I go into the ocean.

Picture a moonless, pitch black night, heavy rain and 20 foot swells. As I surface and get my bearings, I see the sailboat distancing itself from my position. We had equipped the boat with an emergency, portable strobe light attached to a ring buoy that was located on the stern (rearmost part) of the boat. I began yelling "Throw me the buoy". "Throw me the fucking buoy". "Throw me"…. until I was almost hoarse. The rain is beating on my face, the boat is disappearing on the horizon, I have no floatation devices and I am just trying to stay afloat. As the boat reaches about 100 yards from my position, I manage to see the buoy with the strobe light go in the water and now I have to swim for my life. I can taste the salt water and I am running on adrenaline. I haven't exercised in 24 days and I am trying to just keep sight of the buoy in the 20 foot seas. When I reach the buoy I am exhausted. My first thoughts are to pull my sweat pants down over my ankles so that the sharks can't see my bare skin. When I begin to search the horizon I realize the boat is out of sight. We were navigating with a sextant.(an instrument for measuring the angular distance of the sun or star from the horizon. (Webster's definition). Along with a sextant, the positioning calculations were made also using an accurate timepiece, a current almanac and a book called the American Practical Navigator. There was no GPS (global positioning system), no satellite phone, no boat.

Now I take a moment thinking about what I will do next, three days from land in a stormy sea in the pitch black of night.

CHAPTER 2

If you are wondering if life now appears bleak, overwhelming with insurmountable odds you are probably right. I am guessing my chances of winning the lottery were greater than surviving my current situation. If one believes that this situation is hopeless and without choices, then ask this question. Did I survive or is my best friend writing this story on what he believes probably happened 31 years later. If you answered that this situation is hopeless and there are no choices, you probably would have perished the instant you fell off the boat. If you are not sure, you may have made it to the buoy. If you were focused on the task at hand when you reached the buoy, you may have asked yourself where is the boat and how many days can I survive without water. I knew we were still three days from land and the thought of swimming the rest of the way was not out of the question.

The water was warm and even though the storm persisted, I found myself comfortably snug with the horseshoe buoy under my arms. I didn't have to do anything but settle in with the idea that there were choices to be made. It didn't matter what the choices were, I had them and I was going to exercise them. What may have been obvious to some people (just giving up and drowning on the spot) was not even one of my thoughts. Some people over the years have said that I am overly optimistic. I tend to trust others more than I should. I try to start out my day pleasantly and with a smile on my face. I am sure through current satellite technology that if a satellite had been able to look down at me at that very moment, they would have said "Well he's fucked". Obviously, they have not met "Captain Jack".

CHAPTER 3

My favorite sport in early grade school was basketball. I walked to grade school (no it wasn't 5 miles in the snow) and always carried my own, personal basketball. There were no "backpacks" then so choosing to carry a basketball was often challenging. I would try and go early to school so that I could shoot "hoops" before school started. Recess was my favorite class. After school I would go home and then go over to the nearby park to play more basketball. I had a wonderful park behind the house. I could play basketball, ping pong, roller skate and had fun running around avoiding (or not) all of the giant sprinklers. I think my personal basketball may have had a little too much importance. I was riding to school with a neighbor one day and I was sitting next to the right front door of the car. We didn't have seat belts back then. Apparently because I was more interested in holding my basketball than closing the door properly, I created a terrifying moment for our neighbor. As the car made a left turn, my door popped open and out I went out of the car with the basketball. The car wasn't going very fast so I just landed on my feet still clutching this round, orange, inflatable sphere. I was so proud of myself for not dropping that ball. Apparently this is some early behavior of me focusing on something. Yes, I should have focused on shutting the door properly and staying in the car when the door did open. Hey, that basketball was important to me. I don't think that neighbor ever gave me a ride again. Go figure.

CHAPTER 4

I have now been the water about 20 minutes and my thoughts begin to take hold. I am feeling frustrated. I am alone and the darkness is overwhelming. I am in a black hole with nothing in sight. I am losing my sense of time.

CHAPTER 5

When I was in grade school, I was a below average student. I hated to read and was basically "bad" when it came to the reading, writing and arithmetic. I did love one thing. Sports. I played baseball every summer in Little League until I was thirteen. I got so sick of baseball I never went on to play "Babe Ruth". I was fortunate enough to have a 'highlight' in little league that somewhat alleviated my pain of missing all those summers of not doing things that the other kids got to do. You know, like just have time off, go to a few fun places, that sort of thing. I was on a baseball team from Portland Oregon that went to the 1958 World Series in Williamsport, Pennsylvania. We actually had a couple of players that went on to play professional baseball. I remember we ended up in 3rd place.

The other highlight of this trip, so to speak, was meeting a young girl while I was back in Pennsylvania. I think that I was thrilled that a girl actually spoke to me. When I got home from the big baseball adventure there was a letter waiting for me from this particular girl. Before I could open it, my older sister grabbed the letter and locked herself in our downstairs bathroom. My dad had just remodeled it and put on a brand new door. As I was yelling at my sister I was also kicking a hole in the new door. I am 11 years old, never dated yet, and am apparently feeling my new found testosterone (whatever that was). For a reason that totally escapes me (not a clue) at my age, I am convinced that invading my privacy justifies the current action I am now taking. My sister finally opens the door and gives me the unopened letter. Boy, did she have my number. Now the real fear sets in. My dad is going to ground me (again). We had a huge park behind our house and for some reason, I could never come home on time. I was grounded more times than I can remember.

When dad comes home and hears the whole story he did the strangest thing. Before I continue I have to give a description of my father. He was 6 feet 5 inches tall and weighed 250 pounds. I was 5 foot 10 inches tall and weighed 120 pounds. His size was intimidating to say the least. I used to have to stand next to a measuring wall as I was growing up to see if I was going to be taller than my 4 foot 9 inch grandmother. Boy, was my dad relieved when I made it past 5 feet 6 inches. I didn't know what my father's response would have been otherwise. Was this another "grounding" offense?

So my dad hears my story. He totally understands why I did what I did and does not take any negative action. (Is it possible he was a kid once?). He does something else as well. He tells me that I should respect the opposite sex by never sharing information about what happens between a guy and a girl. My mother would come to hate this advice because I took it to the extreme. When my mom would later ask me "how was my evening out on a date", I would politely tell her (as per my dad's previous instructions), "I can't talk about it".

My mom was always supportive and loving towards me. Looking back, I am sure I could have modified my behavior quite a bit. Kids!!

CHAPTER 6

    Somehow I tuned out the noises around me. The darkness is all encompassing and I can feel myself giving into the fear of my predicament. I came to nickname the ocean the "Big O". It was like being in outer space, just drifting along knowing that I am but a subatomic mini-particle in the greater scheme of things. Even though the ocean water was warm, I am starting to feel cold from the dampness. I begin to shiver…. Another 10 minutes goes by.

CHAPTER 7

My junior high school experience consisted of the eighth and ninth grade. I had my father for a basketball coach and also as an industrial arts teacher. My father seemed to be well liked by most everyone and that made it easier for me to kind of blend in.

If I said that I was a "quiet" person that would be an understatement. Growing up I had a sister 3 years older and I believe to this day that she spoke for me for the first few years of my life. I was so quiet that when I ran for student body president my mom didn't know about it until my dad said something to her.

I think I took my life and the events in my life to be placed in the "very personal to be kept to myself category". Any attention brought to myself was of course rewarding but also embarrassing. For the most part, this humility has stayed with me most of my life.

I had plenty of friends growing up and I was more interested in what they had to say than what I had to say. I do remember though, that if a topic was interesting and it wasn't about me, I could actually engage in some lengthy conversations.

This was also a time I found out about my aggressiveness and competitiveness. I learned to channel my aggressiveness through sports. My first week of junior high I was shooting basketballs in the gym and there was this one individual that was "bullying" the other kids. I didn't hit him, but I pushed him away and had a few words. It was so spontaneous I did it without much thought. What the hell was I anyway, the "bully monitor" for the basketball court. Some teachers got involved and put an end to it. I could see I wasn't making a good first impression at school. My dad didn't seem overly concerned so I got through that one alright.

I was not immune to corporal punishment at school, however. I was still a kid and when the class or team did something stupid (like have too much fun), my dad would line us up and paddle our butts. One day in industrial arts class (yes I took my dad's classes), someone put a tack on a mentally challenged student's chair. When my dad heard the outcry from this student he asked for the student that did this to "fess up". Of course nobody did. So guess what? He lined all of us up for the "paddle". As he was going down the line one student cried out particularly loud. My dad has just paddled the victim. The young boy explained "you said for everybody to get in line". My dad just shook his head, finished his paddling, then left the room for a few minutes so he and the class could regain our composure from laughing so hard.

I had discovered that I was pretty good at sports. I was also doing better academically. Everything is my life became competitive. It was the essence of who I was. I hated to lose. It was at this time that I began to focus and pay attention to what I was doing. I would always be an average student. I could accept that. I began to become a leader, not by what I said, but by what I did. It was at this time that I developed stability and composure. It was a calmness that helped keep my teammates focused. It was this focus that would prepare me for the rest of my life…. it would later be challenged in a dark unforgiving sea.

CHAPTER 8

I have heard people say that when threatened with imminent death, their whole life goes through a quick review.

I am not feeling threatened by imminent death. I am in a watery grave and I don't remember having any thoughts of a life review. I am no longer distracted by the darkness, the rain or the 20 foot seas. My struggle now becomes the fear. The real question is, the fear of what? Am I in a hopeless situation? Apparently some people would think so. Is help on the way? Don't have a fucking clue! So now the question may become, why not just give up. Why prolong the inevitable. Am I so willful, so optimistic and so arrogant that I don't consider any of the above options. I know death comes for all of us. I just wasn't ready or willing to give in to it. Why not give up to the notion of a final struggle, at sea alone for days, waiting for the sharks to come and begin feasting. Being just conscious enough to watch as parts of your body are ripped apart. For a moment, the thought crossed my mind to just let go of the buoy, before I was delirious and couldn't make a clear decision later. The situation seemed hopeless as another 10 minutes went by.

CHAPTER 9

Some of my best memories of growing up came from high school. I was involved in sports and in the summers my family would enjoy boating activities on the Columbia River in Portland, Oregon. During my sophomore year we had a basketball team that had three starting sophomores. One played the center position, one a forward, and I was a guard. Our tallest player was 6 feet four and we were considered short by other team's standards. We had our ups and downs and finished the season with more wins than losses. We did not make the high school playoffs.

Our junior year, the now three starting juniors were accompanied by two seniors. We all got along, played hard and didn't have a clue how good we really were. My father had been a high school basketball coach when I was young and had coached one of the most talented teams of the time. I think his team took second in the state basketball finals in Oregon in 1952.

As the season progressed the chemistry really began to take hold among the team members. When we were "running" on all cylinders, the games were not close. When we were struggling, they were close but we managed to win more than lose. Our goal was to get to the high school playoffs. One of our high school teams had made it to the playoffs once before, but were eliminated in the first round.

The last game of the regular season was an away game and we lost. We had been under a lot of pressure during the season and this turned out to be a blessing in disguise. First, it took off a lot of pressure and second, we would be going into the state tournament as the number two team from our conference. It would turn out to be better match up for us. The team collectively was just glad for this upcoming opportunity. We didn't know the challenges ahead, our first goal was just to win one game and then we could feel "proud" of our accomplishments. We were so underrated going into this tournament, I am surprised it didn't have a negative impact on us.

When we arrived at the University of Oregon basketball arena for our first practice for the tournament, you could hear a pin drop. At full capacity, 10,000 people would be watching this little "nobody" team from Parkrose High School in Portland, Oregon.

Our first game was early morning and there were few fans in the stands to watch. We were used to small crowds anyway, even though our high school gym always filled to capacity.

It was a close game but by some miracle (not by our thinking because we didn't know any better), we won. There was a slight mention in the newspaper about an "obscure" team beating one of the many opponents at the tournament. Just a "box" score with no editorial as I remember.

Game number two was close again, but we managed to win another one. This time we got a little editorial besides the "box" score but the "big" press was on the favored team.

When we won the third game, everybody was convinced there was no way we had a chance to defeat the favored team in the tournament for the championship. We were nicknamed "Cinderella" and the sports writers were having a field day writing our "sports obituary" long before the game took place. We were totally okay with the whole idea. We had accomplished more than anyone expected and just making it to the finals was according to just about everyone, a miracle.

Were we excited? Of course. Were we nervous? Absolutely, just like every other game we played. Did we know we were going to lose? Not according to our game plan. If you have ever put together a good plan, stick with it. If you work your plan, you win regardless of the final score.

As we walked onto the floor for our final game of the 1964 season, 10,000 screaming fans were "rocking" the joint. We were so underrated that half the fans were cheering for us out of sympathy. The favored team had made it to the finals and their fans were like the fans in the ancient roman coliseum. These fans were there to watch the slaughter. They believed we didn't even belong in the finals

The game started out with our opposition scoring the first two points. No surprise there. As the game progressed in the first quarter a tension began to build in the arena. Our team was scoring points and the opposition still had their original two points. The opposing fans were in complete shock. The favored team was in complete shock. I think we were in complete shock. The score at the end of the first quarter was 22-2. We had the 22.

No one believed except us that our opposition would not come roaring back to salvage this unbelievable anomaly. At the end of the 3rd quarter we still had a 22 point lead. It wasn't until halfway through the fourth quarter that the fans were beginning to believe the "impossible". Could this "Cinderella" team hold on to actually win the state tournament?

The final score still separated the two teams by 22 points. The impossible, unbelievable, no-way, no-how score told the story. This little "nobody" team had done the impossible. As I look back to these wonderful times, I do remember this. We just focused on what we were doing. We never accepted defeat. We didn't give up just because of what the "critics" said was supposed to happen.

And finally, I do not think we knew any reason why we couldn't win. On whose beliefs should we ever give up, anyway?

Even though I didn't know the significance of it at the time, "Captain Jack" would come to believe there were choices to every situation, even if the things at first seem hopeless.

CHAPTER 10

My sense of everything is numbed by the nothingness around me. Fear now has gripped my entire being. My logic tells me to fight to survive. My emotions are dictating otherwise. Ten more minutes go by.

CHAPTER 11

In 1968 Navy recruiters came to the University of Oregon campus. I knew from the frequent visits that I was making to the Selective Service Board (Draft board) that I would be drafted when I graduated. One day when I was at the student union on campus, I noticed two Navy recruiters had a table set up on the second floor. As I passed by I thought "why not". I was already working on my private pilot license and if I have to serve my country I could do it as an officer and pilot. After a few minutes talking to these really "cool" Navy lieutenants, they suggested I take their qualifying exams. My first concern was if there was any math involved. I was convinced that my high school junior year math teacher was totally wrong when she said "you really need more than Algebra II if you want to go to college. I was getting through college but "boy howdy" was she right about needing math for the Navy. I honestly can't remember if the test was multiple choice, but I do remember completing it. I had no expectations that I would pass the exam but it didn't stop me from taking it.

When I was contacted by the Navy a month later I was overwhelmed with joy to find out I had been accepted into the Navy flight program. What I didn't know until much later was that the military was looking for "expendable" personnel. I'll be damned though to further qualify as "expendable" I still had to take courses in physics, vector analysis and trigonometry to complete my training. Oh, if I had only listened to my high school math teacher.

I just happened to be on campus at the student union later that year and had occasion to see that the Navy recruiters were back. It also happened that day there was a "student protest" regarding the Vietnam war. When I was on the second floor visiting with the Navy personnel there was a mass of students (angry students as I recall) moving toward the Navy recruiters. Somebody in the crowd yelled "Let's throw the baby killers out the window". Getting thrown out of a window is bad enough, but a second story window, no way.

When a protestor grabbed one of the Navy lieutenants, I grabbed the protester and the lieutenant. Now I was not a huge imposing person, but at six feet two and 200 pounds I was not invisible either. I started yelling for the crowd to stop (can't remember my exact words), but I made it clear to the protestors that if the Navy was going through the window, we were all going. At some point, the whole bad idea of throwing Navy personnel out the window got grid-locked. I don't know if the crowd came to its senses or their emotions subsided enough to just be happy burning the American flag that day.

So, the question is, why did I react to that situation the way I did? Thinking back on it, I was just focusing on one thing. Not letting anyone get thrown out of that window. That event took place a long time ago and until now, I have never reflected on it. Was I doing it to be brave? Was there some moral or ethical force behind my actions? Probably the second. Having been the "underdog" most of my life, I guess it was easy to always cheer for and be supportive of "underdog" situations whether it be real life events or sports. This situation was no contest. The Navy men were basically and totally outnumbered. It was not in my sense of "fair play" to stand back and let this happen. I didn't let the situation overwhelm me, I just took an action to get involved and wasn't worried about anything else.

CHAPTER 12

When I went overboard, my wife and friend had their hands full. There had always been the three of us to handle the rough times at sea.

Getting the boat under control was the first priority. After getting the main sail reduced in size, the next order of business was to get the diesel engine started. We had been keeping the battery charged through daily running of the engine. Our fuel supply, however, limited us to the time we could charge the battery each day. Once the motor was started, it was obvious that a great deal of time and distance had separated the boat from where I fell overboard. There would then be a discussion on what to do next…. Start to look for me or continue on to land to get help.

CHAPTER 13

In 1970 I had completed basic jet training in the Navy at the Meridian Mississippi Naval Training Air base. I would start my advanced jet training in a place called Beeville, Texas which is located halfway between San Antonio and Corpus Christi. I had been in the Navy for over a year and a half now so I was kind of getting the hang of the concept "attention to detail". For those of you lucky enough to have had the experience you know what I am talking about. For those of you who have not had the experience, please let me share it with you "in detail", pardon the pun. The items that were subject to such detail were the following:

1. Bed sheets – the top sheet had to be pulled back exactly six inches from the head of the bed.
2. Underwear – Had to be folded exactly six inches square and exactly fit the area from the top sheet to the head of the bed. If underwear did not fit exactly with top bed sheet, then underwear and bed sheet would end up on the floor.
3. Razor blade – Absolutely spotless.
4. Toothpaste tube – No toothpaste on the inside of the cap.
5. Shirts and trousers – No excess threads (referred as Irish pendants) and the shirts and trousers all had to be equally spaced in the hanging area.

Now the whole idea was to transfer our "officer" training to the inside of an aircraft. We did this to the extreme. Every procedure had steps to follow. There was no deviation from this procedure. As I recall one of the emergencies in the aircraft was when the "red" engine fire light came on, the procedure was to eject. Don't bother looking for other indications, just eject. I think the Navy modified this procedure later as the aircraft got more expensive. It really sucked having to eject out of a perfectly good airplane just because of a light malfunction that had nothing to do with an imminent explosion of the engine, the aircraft or the pilot.

One of the major obstacles that I had to overcome was complex. Other pilots were getting killed in the training command. How would I control the fear of that possibility and how would I minimize the chances of getting killed in the training command.

My logic was this. I decided that I would know everything I could possibly know about the aircraft I was flying. Having said that and then doing it was the answer to both of my dilemmas. I figured that if my preparation was good, then what else could I possibly do. Anything beyond that was totally beyond my control. Besides, when you are flying the U.S. Navy's TF9J Cougar nicknamed the "Lead Sled", how bad could it be. Let me think…. I could crash into another airplane…. The engine could quit and I would have to use an ejection seat that literally broke backs when using…. When I landed on the aircraft carrier I could "smack" the fantale (the ass end of the carrier below the flight deck)…. Catapult off the carrier and having many things happen, all bad such as the Steam Catapult was not set high enough to get the aircraft airborne, an engine loss of power or an engine flameout and have the ship run over me…. I think you get the idea.

So here were my choices. Be scared "shitless" every flight or just say "fuck it", I will deal with whatever happens. I took choice number two, I would deal with it.

CHAPTER 14

I have been in the dark ocean now for an hour. I am reflecting on this. I ask myself what has changed. Is the situation now absolutely terrifying? The horseshoe buoy is under my arms so it does not require any strength to keep my head out of the water.

I am bobbing up 20 feet and then down 20 feet. I keep looking for any sign of the boat. I see nothing and can only taste the salt from the windy spray.

CHAPTER 15

In 1976, I was a Washington State trooper driving up and down freeways and other state highways stopping or assisting the motoring public. The job was often more boring than not, but excitement and adventure were always nearby. We were taught early on that there were no "routine" stops so every contact with the public was always friendly, but cautious. We wore the "Smokey the bear" hats and it was always fair game for passing truckers to come close enough to us when we were standing on the roadway to try and blow our hats off. Trying to talk to a motorist and watch for passing vehicles was always an adventure. I don't know if this falls into multi-tasking, but driving down a highway talking on the radio with one hand, holding the steering wheel with the other, memorizing license plate numbers and driving probably way faster than we should was certainly challenging. If I paraphrased this by saying we had to pay attention, that would be an understatement.

On one of my "routine" days I just had lunch with my wife and told her that I would make a quick trip across the town bridge and then call it a day. She was off to work as a Registered Nurse at the local hospital.

The bridge had four lanes with a center divider and I was midway southbound. My attention was drawn to two people waving at me on the opposite side of the bridge. A third person was outside the rail on the water side of the bridge. I turned on my overhead emergency lights, crossed the bridge, made a U-turn, drove back midway across the bridge and parked my car where the three people were located. Before I could reach the railing, the person on the outside of the bridge rail let go and fell about 80 feet to the water. My first thoughts were probably the same as everyone else, there is no way this guy survived. I then saw two interesting things. The river current was actually moving upriver due to the strong ocean tide, and the man rolled over in the water. Now my reaction was to jump in after him. Reason takes over and says "you are out of your fucking mind", go on to choice number two. I noticed a building under construction up river which afforded a place that I could park my patrol car and swim out to get to this man. I jump in my car, advise dispatch of what I am doing and request assistance. When I park my car, I got out, took off my gunbelt, shirt and shoes, locked my car and entered the water. I noticed constructions workers off to my left on top of a new Walmart building and later found out what reaction they had to me entering the water.

("what the fuck"?). I started swimming and didn't notice that I had cut my right foot as I entered the water. I didn't have a clue that my swim to get to the victim was going to be around 250 yards. I did know that if I got into trouble, I could use my trousers as a floatation device by tying the legs together and then filling them with air.

About halfway there I was getting very tired. The wind had picked up and the water was choppy. Now I start thinking that I am making this swim to recover a "dead man". When I get close enough to the body I notice it is face down in the water. I am exhausted, I swam all this way for no reason, and now I have to roll over a body whose lifeless form saddens me. The only other time that I have touched "dead" bodies is at car accident scenes to see if there is any pulse. I hesitate….

I reach out to him and roll him over. Bubbles are blowing from his mouth. I can't believe it. His life has given me renewed strength to try and get him back to shore. I keep him on his back, grab the back of his jacket collar with my right hand to keep his head out of the water, and scissor kick back towards the shore. When I am about 25 yards from shore, a ring buoy is tossed to me. When I am pulled into a dock area, I help the man up so he could be given CPR. Before I could tell the other officer to use something to cover the victim's mouth before beginning, it was too late. The victim had regurgitated a good deal of the Chehalis River all over this well-intended officer.

The victim was sent to the local hospital to recover. I noticed that my Sergeant had appeared on the scene and I asked him to unlock my patrol car. He noticed that I am limping and offered me a ride. I was probably not thinking too clearly at the time and said I will just drive myself to the hospital. I had been to the emergency room several times to see my wife who worked in "ER" or to follow up on accident reports many times in the past. When I came walking into ER with no shoes, a T-shirt, no gun and sopping wet I got the strangest looks. Once I explained the foot injury, I was admitted. My wife had a be-mused look on her face as I explained to her what happened. She later took care of the gentlemen who did survive but would have no memory of jumping off the bridge. As my right foot was getting stitched in the Emergency Room I got a visit from my Sergeant and our Lieutenant. The Lieutenant proceeded to "Chew my ass" for doing such a stupid thing. I found out later that he had lost a fellow officer and friend trying to make a water rescue. I have to say, though that this was not uncommon for Troopers who had just assisted accident victims to get "chewed" out by senior officers. A senior officer shows up on a scene and notices the trooper's shoes are dirty and he is not wearing his hat. It was a definite traditional "no-no" to not be wearing your hat unless indoors. Never mind that this same trooper just helped out another accident victim. For my actions that day, I became the first Washington State Patrol recipient of the Award of Honor, given by the Governor of the state of Washington. There had been 88 previous nominations for this award.

CHAPTER 16

I was employed with the Washington State Patrol just prior to taking the sailboat trip to Hawaii and then after my educational leave of absence I returned to work for the patrol.

In my youth I was probably as "reserved" as everyone else. I also had an ingrained sense of fairness and really believed that advancement in life came with the quality of each of us as a person and our experiences. I always understood what diplomacy was. I also understood that more often than not, politics was the driving force behind (as far as I was concerned), way too many decisions.

In order for me to make possible our sailboat trip to Hawaii, I took some actions (not related to the trip) that as it would turn out, were not "politically" correct.

I had applied for an opening in the Washington State Patrol's Aviation unit. With my previous Navy experience as an Aviator, I was the most qualified applicant. I had been previously interviewed by the Aviation Division Commander and he told me I was the most qualified pilot at the time. I knew who the other applicants were and none of them had the experience that I did. More important than experience, though was compatibility. Compatibility was and still is the number one criteria to consider any applicant. Not truly understanding compatibility and seniority at the time, I found myself going down a path I had traveled before. I couldn't stand politics in the Navy, and now it was happening to me again, politics were all over this one. The good old boy network, was alive and well.

CHAPTER 17

When I was not given the position in the Washington State Patrol Aviation Division, I was frustrated and angry. I was so angry that I wrote a letter to the Chief of the Patrol explaining my position as I saw it. How can I be told I am the most qualified person for the job and not get it. That was the first nail in my coffin. Politics was raising its ugly head, and I didn't have a clue to the path I was now on. Hadn't I just become the State Patrol's first recipient of the Award of Honor? Wasn't my job performance equal or better than my peers?

When I received what I considered a "patronizing" response to my situation, I put the second nail in my coffin. After several discussions with my family and fellow troopers, enough fuel had been added to the fire for me to turn in my resignation.

The reaction I got was interesting. My sergeant took the letter and read it. He had no comments at all for me. I heard nothing from my lieutenant or my district captain.

Twenty nine and a half days, one half day before I was to turn in all of my equipment, I get a call from the lead trooper representative in the state. The statement he presented me was this. "Your fellow troopers do not want you to leave the patrol. If I can get the Chief of the Patrol to call you, will you take the call? My response was, "I haven't heard from anyone in twenty nine and one half days, if the Chief wants to talk to me, he can call me before the end of my last shift, which is today." I got the call ten minutes later.

The Chief of the Patrol had been the head of the State Patrol academy when I attended that joyful event almost two years earlier. I had always found him to be fair and a good listener. He wasn't willing to change the decisions that had been made reference the Aviation position, but he did listen. He was willing to send one of his Major's down the next day to try and see if we could possibly move forward without me leaving the patrol. I agreed.

One of my many frustrations (those of you who have worked for government know what I mean) that I had was trying to get an educational leave of absence. The patrol's position of using my Veteran's benefits for getting additional flight training, would not qualify.

CHAPTER 18

I met with the Major mid-morning the next day. It was obvious from my conversation that the patrol was listening. I knew the major loved to sail so I shared my dream of sailing to Hawaii, using my Veteran's benefits that would pay for 90 percent of my flight training, etc. I was told that he would get back to me in a timely manner. Within a couple of days, I did hear back from the major and my request was to be approved. I felt a reasonable compromise had been made. You know that Einstein theory of relativity about an "equal and opposite reaction"? That may be true in physics, but not in politics. The patrol was going to make me pay, big time for asking something outside of the normal rules and regulations. The final nail in the coffin was waiting for me, I just didn't know it yet. If history repeats itself, I was going to get "pissed off" all over again.

CHAPTER 19

An hour and a half has gone by since I fell overboard. I am wet, frustrated and have no energy left to deal with my current situation. It was then that I make some decisions.

I choose not to deal with the fear anymore. I choose not to let my dilemma incapacitate me. I choose not to give up. Then the question becomes, why not?

The answer becomes clear and simple...Because I have decided to make peace with myself. I will make peace with the ocean. I will make peace with the sharks. I will make peace with the universe. I will take myself to a place of rapture.

As if in a dream, I am transported to this place of ecstasy or rapture. I am not delirious nor am I unconscious. I made a choice. There is nothing around me nor anyone to help me. At that very moment, I helped decide my own fate. Did I save myself? No. I gave myself the opportunity to be saved. I reached out and touched the "Hand of God".

My life and being as I had known it were changing. It was as if all my preconceived notions and objections were being removed. The impossible was now the possible. I am in such a state of euphoric mind and body that there is nothing but bliss. Have I transcended to another plain of consciousness? Do I not know what is real or what is unreal? What was before me was the choice that I had all along. It is the same choice everyone has all the time. It is always there, for all of us. Sometimes we have to forget ourselves, or get out of our own way to remember it. The best way I can describe the feeling that I had was a powerful connection with the "Universe"; a presence touching me and letting me know that I was okay.

I knew that I was okay. I wish I could explain what that means. There was no boat in sight. The only thing that changed was me.

As I refocused in my peaceful state another half hour had gone by. I am still in the water and don't have a clue from which direction the boat would come.

Then, I think I see a light off in the distance. It is a mast light and it is heading somewhat in my direction.

I am now trying to hold my strobe light over my head. They don't see me. I immediately lose my "bliss". I can't fucking believe it.

Like an idiot, I am trying to yell and be heard over the howling winds. As the boat is about to disappear from my sight a second time…. it turns in my direction. They now see the strobe. I am and always have been, okay.

Not realizing until years later, as a result of this experience, John Taylor Mulder had been transformed into "Captain Jack". Now the real adventure begins.

CHAPTER 20

We had reached Hawaii in November of 1977. By April 1978, I was ready to go back to the state patrol. We decided to sell our sailboat in Hawaii and fly home commercially. Five and a half hours was sure a lot quicker than 27 days.

My logic told me when I got back to the Washington State Patrol I would go right into the Aviation division. My emotions knew better. I had been living in Western Washington for some time. I figured the worst that could happen was that I would at least be stationed near Olympia (where the aircraft were located), working the road so that I could be next in line for any future aviation openings. You know what they say about expectations. I got sent to a little town of 500 people near the northeast Washington border.

Here came the first of the "shit" and I could be sure of more. What the patrol didn't know was that they were now dealing with "Captain Jack".

CHAPTER 21

We got settled into this very friendly community and I was going about my business again of being a trooper on the road. My wife took a job at a hospital in a nearby town. I hadn't given up on the aviation idea, but I had other plans in mind. I applied to and got accepted to the Master's program at Gonzaga University in Spokane, Washington. But most importantly, my daughter was born. "Captain Jack" as a father, how cool was that!

Before I started school, another opening became available in the aviation division. This opening just happened to be in Moses Lake, Washington flying traffic patrol. I decided to apply once again, knowing this time that logic would surely take hold over emotion this time.

There were four applicants applying for the position. The minimum qualifications were clearly stated. One of the applicants had not completed one of the qualifications, but got hired for the job anyway. Okay, what was wrong with this picture and how did I respond to it? Must have been that compatibility thing again. Let me see, my two nails in the coffin against one unqualified applicant. I really had "pissed off" the Aviation commander with that letter I had sent.

Having been served payment "number 2" from the state patrol did not get the previous response from me as before. The Jack Mulder that went into the water was not the same Jack Mulder that came out. This new person called "Captain Jack" was looking at better choices now. I simply picked up the phone and thanked the aviation commander for the opportunity to interview. I had transformed my "dislike" for politics into what would become my "art" of diplomacy. Of course what I thought was art was also perceived by some as pure "bullshit". But at least it was pure, it worked and I could live with it.

CHAPTER 22

Starting school at Gonzaga was still months away and an interesting turn of events took place. There was a radio broadcast that a state patrol aircraft had clipped some power lines near Yakima, Washington and thankfully, no one was hurt. This incident took place before a mass of media "kicking off" a 55 mph speed limit campaign using the aircraft and ground troopers in patrol cars. The aircraft had special watches calibrated in miles per hour that would time vehicles between half mile and mile marks on the roadways.

The state patrol aircraft had apparently made a couple of low passes at the request of the media. They wanted a lower pass and "boy" did they get it. One of the troopers riding along in the aircraft later wrote an article titled "30 seconds over Yakima" which included vivid detail of the aircraft propeller cutting through power lines.

A day later I got a call from one of my trooper friends pretending to be the chief of the patrol asking me if I wanted to go into the aviation division now. He had me going for a minute. I called him a "son of a bitch", we laughed and he hung up. Ten minutes later I get a call from my district captain asking me to meet with the chief about an aviation position. I think my response was "who is this and you are full of shit". It really was my district captain and when I told him what had just happened he laughed with me.

The Federal Aviation Administration had just suspended our eastern Washington pilot and now I was getting the call to consider the position. I had been told after my last interview that there would eventually be two troopers assigned to eastern Washington, but now this was occurring a little earlier than was expected. I knew there were other applicants out there besides me. I guess desperate times call for desperate measures. I already lived in eastern Washington and apparently that final nail in the coffin would get put back on the shelf if I did just one thing. I was not to write any more nasty letters to the Chief.... I could live with that, at least for now.

CHAPTER 23

The State Patrol's aircraft enforcement program was about to transform. For years there had been one small aircraft (Cessna 182 which was a single engine high wing aircraft) patrolling the entire state. That aircraft had been based in Olympia, Washington.

With Federal funding, a second aircraft (another Cessna 182) was to be based in eastern Washington at the Moses Lake airport. The Olympia based aircraft was mostly used when the transportation aircraft (twin engine turboprop King Airs) were not in service. The King Airs were used for the transportation of the Governor and other state personnel.

Once I got all checked out in the Cessna which now included not just flying the aircraft, but holding a calibrated stop watch in each hand, (a watch that was started when a vehicle passed one mark on the highway and stopped when it passed a second mark) talking to the troopers on the ground, talking to air traffic control and watching out for other aircraft, the real fun had begun. With two trooper pilots now in service in eastern Washington, we were "turned loose" on the motoring public. We were going to get serious about stopping all those "speeders" that were exceeding the "55" mile per hour speed limit. We did not have a quota system as many people believed and our enforcement was fair because it clocked a vehicle's average speed over a half mile or mile distance. If it was a busy day we probably did not call out anyone for going less than 10 miles per hour over the speed limit. If it was a slow day, we may have called out vehicles going eight miles over the speed limit and they would get a warning. If there was only one vehicle on the highway (I am not kidding), we would probably have them stopped just to see if they were lost. (I am kidding).

There were two memorable aircraft stops that come to mind. One was a vehicle traveling 136 miles an hour. He thought he evaded us when he got off the highway and hid behind a building. Boy was he surprised when troopers pulled up behind him and just pointed up. The other stop just happened to be an out of state vehicle. The driver demanded to see the judge immediately. We had to land the aircraft and get a ride to the courthouse. When the judge listened to our testimony about aircraft enforcement (for the 100th time) he couldn't help but chuckle. The driver of the out of state vehicle thought that we were intentionally going after out of state vehicles and that we could actually read license plate numbers and from which state the vehicle was from at 1500 feet above the ground. Being able to do that would be an incredible feat. To then identify that license plate as being out of state was just not possible. Case closed.

My partner in eastern Washington was compatible, had a great sense of humor, and together we set new standards of performance when it came to the number of stops we were able to facilitate by aircraft. Within a month we exceeded the previous number of stops for any given day or month. By the end of the year, we had stopped more vehicles than the Olympia based aircraft had stopped in the previous four years. We were nicknamed the "dynamic duo". We had way too much fun.

When an opening became available in the aviation division in Olympia to fly the King Air aircraft, I was asked to take the position. It was May of 1980. This new person "Captain Jack" had behaved himself "politically" and once again, was the most qualified pilot for the position. My excellent job performance was probably considered in there somewhere, too. It was sad leaving my partner, but his turn to move to Olympia would be forthcoming.

CHAPTER 24

May of 1980 was a challenging month for the Washington State Patrol. Mt. St. Helens had been showing signs of a possible eruption. The State Patrol had just equipped its Cessna 182's with external public address systems to help direct people on the ground when necessary.

Just prior to the May 18th eruption of the mountain, our State Patrol chief had made a personal visit to Spirit Lake to talk to a gentleman (I believe his name was Harry Truman) into leaving his lodge. Harry politely refused and would soon disappear forever, but never forgotten.

On May 18th, I had boarded a commercial flight from Spokane, Washington for Wichita, Kansas to begin my King Air Initial training. My flight connected through Denver so when I arrived at my first stop I called my wife. What she was about to tell me had me very concerned and for the most part, feeling helpless. My wife had told me that Mt. St. Helens had just erupted. At noon, mountain ash had totally darkened the sky. News reports were warning everyone to stay indoors and to put wet towels around the doors and windows. There was concern that the ash cloud may be toxic.

I immediately called my boss in Olympia to see about catching a flight back to Spokane. He assured me the "black cloud" was not toxic and that the state patrol had a trooper on the way to check on my wife. Getting a flight back to Spokane was not going to happen anyway, as many flights were being cancelled. I continued on to Wichita to start my training.

On the day that Mt. St. Helens erupted, the Olympia based Cessna 182 had been dispatched to an area just west of the mountain to an area over the Toutle River. Several fisherman were unaware of the debris and raging flood waters that were heading their way. Because the aircraft had public address speakers, a broadcast was able to warn the fisherman to get off the river. Being able to assist the public was always one of the best parts of the job.

Washington State was in chaos. I remember calling my boss several times asking if I should come back to assist, but he thought it best I go ahead and finish school. There was plenty to do when I got back (no shit). Knowing that my family was cared for gave me the peace of mind to finish school and then return home.

When I returned to Spokane, I thought I had landed in a strange country. This "ash" from Mt. St. Helens was everywhere. Try to picture a 3 to 4 inch snowfall except it was gray and it was not going to melt. Its consistency was so fine it was like "talcum" powder. If you tried and wash it away, it turned into "muck" or a heavy semi-solid mass. It took snow removal equipment to remove it from the streets. It would take homeowners a long time to remove it from their roofs. All the farmers were in total "panic" that their crops were ruined. Driver's actually put coffee filters in with their air filters to help keep the ash out of their engines.

I would be moving to Olympia in a week but got to observe some of nature's "wonder". All the plants in our back yard had flourished and had grown at an incredible rate. To everyone's surprise, the ash from Mt. St. Helens was an incredible nutrient and the farmers of eastern Washington had their best crop ever.

CHAPTER 25

My first month living in Olympia was not dull. My daughter was fourteen months, my wife was trying to get our house organized and I was adjusting to my new position. Working in eastern Washington had gone very smoothly. There had just been the two pilots working together and we had spent so much time in the aircraft that we could anticipate each other's next move.

Working in Olympia was going to be a whole new challenge. The aviation division was somewhat (actually a whole lot) dysfunctional. Now remember that I came from a navy background where "order" was the rule. You know what the saying was "there was nothing worse than an "ex" something. Well I was "ex" navy and I was convinced that my way was the "true" path to aviation enlightenment. My point of view was actually just as fucked up as the aviation division was dysfunctional. Finding the solution would be a journey we would all remember. So for a few of my fellow pilots in the state patrol, I apologize to you for thinking you were "Richard craniums" (dickheads). Actually there was a "Dick" in our group but that was a whole "nother" story.

CHAPTER 26

My very first King Air flight was with my boss flying the then Governor of Washington, Dixie Lee Ray. We had to fly from Olympia down to Kelso, Washington so that our Governor could meet with a state senator from Oregon regarding Mt. St. Helens.

The weather had been overcast that day so we had to depart Kelso on and "instrument" flight plan. This involved having to talk to an air traffic controller to get permission to fly into the clouds. I was the second pilot in the right seat and my job, my one and only job was to talk on the radios. So once again, I am off to a great start. On the dial that changes the radio frequencies was also the on-off switch. After takeoff and into the clouds I switch the radio frequency and because I turned the dial to the left instead of to the right, I unknowingly turned off the radio. There is a procedure that is taught in aviation that once you do something that was followed by something undesirable, simply undo what was just done. For us it wasn't quite that simple, but we did figure it out. What a way to start my first flight. Politics aside, the Governor was always friendly to the aviation group and knew each of us by name.

CHAPTER 27

My first opportunity to see Mt. St. Helens came on an overcast day. I had to pick up a sergeant from our Kelso office and fly him up to the mountain in one of our Cessna 182's. Both of us had seen newspaper and televised pictures of the damage, but this was our first glimpse in person.

As I approached the first noticeable damage, I felt like I had just come upon a lunar landscape. Everything was the color gray. The normal tree-line just stopped. Next to the tree-line were thousands of trees laying horizontally on the ground. They looked like a thousand "toothpicks" in some kind of chaotic order. (Yes that is an oxymoron). I didn't know how else to describe it.

After the fallen trees, there was just gray barren landscape. It was eerie to say the least. It was at most beyond shocking to see this kind of destruction. We continued our journey, first seeing what was left of Spirit Lake, then seeing Mt. St. Helens with the whole side of the mountain missing with this white plume coming out of the base. I made more than 20 trips to the mountain and each time it had the same effect on me. I was always awestruck and so were my passengers. I just don't have the words to describe it.

CHAPTER 28

After about six months in Olympia, I saw a pattern that was all too familiar. My fellow pilots were not too motivated, probably bored with their jobs and were beginning to feel it was "beneath" them to have to fly the single engine aircraft. After all, they were part of an elite group that flew the Governor and other dignitaries around.

Since I was the low person in seniority, I did two things. The first was just to stick to my own work ethic and do my job the best that I could. The second was to ascertain why my fellow pilots were so unhappy.

By sticking to my work ethic, I probably made some of my co-workers uncomfortable. I had no problem taking a mop and bucket and cleaning the hangar floor. My co-workers would find other things to do (like disappear).

When I said earlier that the aviation division was dysfunctional, it was for the following reasons. All the training that had been received had been "in house". In house training can be a good thing, but because the aviation division had a limited budget for any training, it was often sporadic and inconsistent.

Each King Air was flown by two pilots. Each crew consisted of a "pilot in command or PIC" and a "second in command or SIC". Sounds good so far, right? What happened in the aircraft during a flight was anybody's guess. There were "PIC's" who wanted to do everything in the cockpit. There were "PIC's" that divided the cockpit saying, "this was my side and that was your side. The SIC was not to cross that imaginary line or touch any switches that the PIC had deemed to be in his control. Talk about "negative cockpit resource management". The SIC would often not tell the PIC if he missed a switch or a particular procedure in the aircraft. The flight became an "egofest" to see which side of the cockpit made fewer mistakes, and then the "fewer mistakes pilot" could "rag" on the other pilot afterwards. And then there were PIC's that actually wanted to work together as a crew. These crew variations were not unlike the airlines at the time, either. We were so "unprofessional" it was disconcerting and embarrassing.

Finally the funding became available for outside training in an actual aircraft simulator. This was a device that had exactly the same switches and displays as the aircraft, had motion, and one could experience all kinds of emergencies without the normal fear associated with it. My boss and I just happened to be the first to go to this training. I now had to show my boss (yes the same one that got the letter) my level of competency and I would get to see his. By my calculations, the pressure was just as much on him than it was on me. We both survived the experience and I came out with a better understanding of my boss.

The second reason was more subtle. Only two of the six pilots had achieved the advanced pilot rating called "Airline Transport". The airline transport rating in aviation was the highest rating one can achieve and was the same rating that airline captains had. None of us except the aviation commander and one of our lieutenants had this qualification. I personally thought it would not only help the morale of the unit, but it was a level the unit should have anyway. After all, the aviation unit was a prestigious billet getting to fly the Governor around and we should have the most qualified pilots taking that responsibility. There I go again, talking about qualified pilots.

We had a good group except for a couple of pilots that were very unhappy. One was an older, unhappy pilot that was getting close to retirement and had some health issues (often fell asleep on the King Air flights). Passengers asked if this pilot was okay and we would say something like, late night, etc. The other pilot was a younger, unhappy uncomfortable pilot in a job that he really didn't want.

After several flights with the younger unhappy pilot, I finally had to ask him why he was still flying. He admitted to having stress and stomach problems and would eventually leave the aviation division for another position. He ended up in the "Bomb" squad and absolutely loved it. I am still trying to figure that one out.

CHAPTER 29

By 1983 all of our King Air pilots had achieved the Airline Transport Ratings. It was hard work for all of us, but we took ourselves to the highest level of aviation qualification.

The year 1983 was good for me as well. My son was born, I was in my first quarter of graduate school at Evergreen college in Olympia and I was a Pilot in Command in the King Airs. Then another unusual event took place.

The assistant aviation commander got transferred out of the division. Now we had a "captain" in charge of the unit and the rest of us were troopers. We had no sergeants or lieutenants.

The State Patrol powers to be decided to open a position for assistant aviation commander to any sergeant within the state patrol. By opening the position to all employees would meet any "state" regulations when it came to hiring. I was asked by my boss to submit a resume even though I was not a sergeant at the time. Rules didn't seem to matter in the past so what the hell.

I, once again, knew that I was the most qualified for the position and I was now acclimated to the "politics" around me. The "Captain Jack" in me also knew that I would not be writing any "negative" letters should I not get the position.

Within a month, the decision had been made. I got a call at my residence one morning congratulating me. When my boss said "congratulations lieutenant", I had to ask my boss to repeat that.

Apparently the state patrol felt the position of assistant aviation commander should be held by a lieutenant, not a sergeant. I was told to report to a deputy chief's office so that I could be properly instructed on "how to conduct" myself in this position. The state patrol's motto was "service with humility" and by golly I was expected to be humble. I was confident and still reserved, I could be nothing else. The position would not change that. I did tell my mom about the promotion. I think she was equally pleased that I was promoted and also that I was willing to share that with her. With two young children in the household and a new position, I decided not to continue with graduate school. I had enough on my plate and I did not want to miss any more of my children's time than I had to.

If you haven't figured me out yet, I can help with that. I was confident, professional and reserved to the point where I almost never shared any information about who I was except for my closest friends and family. My lifetime friend to be made it his mission in life to consistently remind me "It's okay to tell people about yourself". As reserved as I was, I still felt like it was presumptuous of me to tell people about events in my life. Good or bad, my father's words about keeping things to myself would be a constant challenge. It was always a struggle to find a comfortable balance.

CHAPTER 30

My best friend to be had recently been hired by the state patrol as a civilian consultant to do three things. One was to re-organize all the employee files and purge any information that was not pertinent. Number two was to write a sexual harassment policy. We had female troopers now and we had to conform to state and federal policy. Number three was to help with minority hiring.

My friend was over-qualified for the work that he was asked to do. He was smart, he had experience and he was black. His best quality was in understanding other people. He was older than I was and his insight became invaluable to me. In years to come, we would become invaluable to each other.

My best friend wrote the sexual harassment policy for the state patrol that is probably still in effect to this day (you know how slow government change is). He was also instrumental in giving me some tools to transition from trooper to lieutenant.

To go from trooper one day to lieutenant the next had some interesting challenges. I had been an officer in the navy so I understood certain protocol. I had also been a supervisor in the navy and I knew how to be fair and respectful. I needed to address the "acceptance" issue that my fellow troopers had with having one of their own become "one of them". I also needed to establish guidelines for the pilot group. All but two of my fellow troopers accepted me in my new position. Those close to me understood that I was an advocate for those working with me. Notice I said those working with me, not for me. Leadership for me was not about words, but appropriate actions to help ensure outcomes that were best for everyone.

The two other troopers in my group were a little different. They were both older and more senior to me as far as longevity with the state patrol went. One of the pilots was the one that had been hired on my first attempt to get into the aviation division. We had some friction for a number of other reasons and I knew this individual felt I would make his life miserable now that I was his supervisor. He actually initiated a meeting to make "peace" with me. He stated that he was in total support of my new position and he would like to put any old "issues" to rest. He was sincere and I believed him. I then gave him the responsibility as training officer in the Cessna aircraft. He was a good instructor and he deserved it. We got along just fine after that.

The other trooper and I had got along just fine until my promotion. Because he was "senior" and older he felt he should have been the one promoted. Everything to him was either "black or white", nothing in between. He was to be a challenge until the day he retired.

I am sure the other state patrol officers had mixed feelings about my promotion as well. There was envy, jealousy, and I am sure some bewilderment at this newly promoted lieutenant. Wasn't this the same person that received the "award of honor"? Wasn't this the same person that wrote the "letter"? What strange and confusing politics! I couldn't agree more.

From my point of view I just had to focus (there is that word again) on a few important issues. I had to continue to just be "myself", do my job and continue to learn how to survive in this complicated "political" arena.

CHAPTER 31

By 1984 I was comfortably enjoying my job. My boss had been given an additional assignment as "legislative liaison" for the state patrol. He was busy lobbying for budgets and other state patrol needs. I still answered to him, but for the most part I was responsible for the day to day operations in the aviation division.

Every once in a while someone in the state patrol would ask me about sailing to Hawaii. They would always seem interested and awed by the experience. After seven years, no one outside of my immediate family and friends knew about me going overboard. Up to this point, my experience was off limits, too personal and too emotional to discuss.

It wasn't until a trip I took with my boss did I venture beyond my "comfort" zone. We had gone to Phoenix, Arizona for a couple of days. One afternoon we were sitting by the pool side enjoying a cocktail.

Somehow the conversation steered toward my Hawaii trip. He seemed to be very interested so I began to tell the story. When I got to the point just before overboard, I did something I had not done with an "outsider" before. I began to share a modified version of my "overboard" experience.

Questions were coming faster than I could answer them. If you had ever told a story and wondered if you had the listener's attention, my boss was riveted.

Still too personal and emotional to talk about the "rapture" part, I did finish the story.

…. As the boat was approaching my position in the water, I felt a number of emotions. I felt a sense of relief, I felt a sense of clarity and I was angry. What could I possibly be angry about after spending two hours in a dark stormy sea and then be rescued?

As I climbed back aboard the boat, I was cold and shivering. I hugged my wife and could feel her sense of relief. She would later remind me of the Saint Christopher medal she had given me that I wore around my neck. Was I angry because I had to leave the ocean, this place of rapture and peacefulness? Looking back, I think I was angry because it took so long for my wife and friend to get the buoy with the strobe light in the water. I was angry because I had to face my own mortality. I was angry because I did not understand how I survived.

After stating my anger regarding the time it took to get the buoy in the water to my wife and friend, I didn't want to talk about what had just happened. I asked my friend to continue motoring on our continuous magnetic course of 240 degrees and I went below deck to get on some dry clothes. I now remember my wife throwing that black "T" shirt and dark sweatpants away. Reality was setting in, and it was too uncomfortable to want to revisit it.

On the boat the following morning I remember my mood was quiet and reflective. My wife and friend knew better or were too uncomfortable themselves to want to revisit the night before. Of course I was thankful that they had found me. Maybe I was feeling the loss of the person that fell in the ocean and was struggling with my new identity. Maybe the whole event was so traumatic the concept of absorbing it was well beyond my capacity. Maybe being at sea for 24 days was getting to all of us.

In the afternoon of the 25th day we thought we saw land in the distance. All of our moods changed instantly. As we continued westward into the clearing skies, what we saw was not land, simply clouds that looked like land. All three of us "emotionally" went from the peak of exhilaration to the depth of despair. Hadn't we been through enough already? Did we miss the Hawaiian Islands and now had to wait weeks more to run into the Asian coast? Once again, I had to focus on our course and believe in my calculations. We had enough food for 6 months and ample water for another month. The question became, how much longer could we deal with the sea?

We continued the 26th day pretty much with the same routine as before. Every day would start out with everyone meeting on deck around 6:am in the morning for coffee and conversation. Our friend would then go forward to his sleeping area and catch up on some sleep. My wife and I would do the morning dishes. We found that salt water and Ivory soap worked really well in a bucket. Every once in a while I would forget to look in the bucket before I threw the dish water overboard and we would lose some utensils.

Our routine always gave us something to look forward to. By noon we did our "sextant" calculations and then had lunch and for the first half of the trip we were able to listen to Casey Casem on a Los Angeles radio station. When we were able to tune in to a Hawaiian radio station it was a cause for excitement and celebration.

During the day it was always pleasant to read and enjoy the sailing during a fair wind day. On no wind days, the boat would gently rock and the boom would "clang" back and forth providing us with an annoying sound. It was like a baby crying with no way to comfort it.

The afternoons were spent pretty much the same way. Boat repairs were made and general cleanup took place. It was often warm enough for salt water showers. Yes the bucket again.

CHAPTER 32

After I returned from Phoenix, Arizona with my boss, I resumed my duties and everything was back to normal, or so I thought.

When I had shared my overboard experience with my boss, I never gave it a thought that my story would go any further. Apparently at one of my boss's staff meetings, he had shared my experience with some of his peers. There was a saying in the patrol "Teletype, telephone, tell a trooper". It always amazed me how fast "gossip" traveled within the state of Washington.

I didn't have a clue this had happened until one day I was approached by a "major" boarding one of my flights. He came up to me and said "I heard about your going overboard on your trip to Hawaii. You have to be the luckiest son of a bitch in the world. From now on, I am only going to fly when you are on board. Talking about getting blindsided. At first I was speechless. I had more emotions going through me than I could possibly track. There was privacy, what about my privacy? Well, I didn't tell my boss not to say anything. There was a moment of a flashback to that dark night. Then I think the "Captain Jack" part of me took over. I think my response was "Well, thank you Major, I will do the best I can to take care of you". My next thought as I made my way to the cockpit was simply "Well I'll be damned".

I still laugh about that comment today. The only thing that I had done in the ocean was to change my attitude about my circumstances. My wife and friend, God, and the universe determined the rest. If the forces of the universe wanted to end my life on my very next flight, those were circumstances totally out of my control. I had no way of trying to explain "that" to the major.

CHAPTER 33

Looking back at my job in the state patrol most people would agree that I had a "dream" job, but it wasn't enough. I had a bright future and knew that some day I would be totally in charge of the aviation division.

I would never be satisfied with that. I had already put my name in for the Chief of the state patrol position when there was a change in Governors. Not even getting an interview did not bother me. I had clarity in regard to staying employed by the state of Washington which I will share in the following statement:

Most state employees were competent, quality individuals. The government system inherently protected the weak and limited the opportunities of its most promising members. Through my 12 years with the state patrol, myself and others had ideas for promising change. That was what motivated myself and others. When the reality set in that the "government" did not want change, my choice became simple. It was time for "Captain Jack" to move on. It was time for the next adventure.

CHAPTER 34

With change came a move to San Francisco, California. I would get bitten by the "adventure" bug one more time.

A friend of mine had come up with an opportunity to fly a DC-3 (Douglas C-47 World War II cargo plane) in Alaska. He and I flew to Anchorage, Alaska to meet with a Native American council who controlled their own entities. The meeting was brief but positive, and we would return a couple of months later. We would "partner" up with a group of former "Air America" pilots and a former "Delta" force commando that operated C-119 (flying boxcar) aircraft out of Anchorage. Yes, this was a fascinating group of people. Our role with the DC-3 aircraft was to fly the smaller loads of cargo to the more remote landing strips that were too small for the C-119's.

My friend was able to acquire the DC-3 aircraft and we found a qualified pilot to go with us until I could get checked out in the DC-3. Although my ocean going experience was a "once in a lifetime" adventure, this was an opportunity to experience the "last frontier". Every flight would indeed be an adventure, and once again, that would be an understatement.

CHAPTER 35

I met this particular friend when he was a 19 year old steam plant worker in Hoquiam, Washington. I was a trooper working the road at the time. He used to drive his 1967 silver Corvette along the Westport-Aberdeen highway. The very first time I stopped him was because his car was missing a front license plate. This young lad explained to me that the front bumper was in repair and that he would replace the plate as soon as the repair was made. I gave him a written warning and went on my way.

About two weeks later, I noticed the vehicle again still without a front plate. When this individual saw that I was turning around he just pulled over to the side of the road and waited for me. Once again, I asked him about the front plate and suggested that he could just attach it with some wire. This kid had a great sense of humor. He was into fixing up classic cars and the thought of using "baling wire" to attach a front license plate was beyond his comprehension. You would think I just said something "sacra religious", and in car terms, I probably had. This routine was repeated several times and each time I stopped this young man the more we would talk. Finally, after about the 5th stop he said to me "you have stopped me so many times why don't you just buy this car". The thought had never crossed my mind. "Okay, I will", I said, "but first you have to get that front license plate attached. He did and I bought the car. Our friendship had formed.

CHAPTER 36

My time in Alaska was from June through September. I was one of the fortunate Alaska pilots that never had to endure the cold, brutal and unforgiving winters.

For the type of trips that we were making, we were putting about 7,500 pounds of cargo on per trip. Sometimes we would do two trips per day. We did not have cargo handlers or loaders. Two or three of us would load this cargo by hand every day. A DC-3 aircraft is a "tail-dragger" aircraft which meant that once the cargo was placed in the aircraft, we had to hand winch it uphill. The physical labor aside, the flights were always fascinating. Getting around Alaska often involved very low altitude flying, some over rugged terrain and some into some very small villages. It was always exhilarating and the Native people were always glad to see us. On one flight after unloading the cargo, we got our picture taken with a father and son. The smile on that young man's face was endearing.

On another flight we actually landed on a beach at Egigik, Alaska. Taking off on a sandy beach was a thrill in itself.

One flight we ended up in Kotzebue, just inside the Arctic circle. This was in a DC-7 aircraft that we could lease on a flight per flight basis. I have never seen so many fresh salmon in one place, around 20,000 pounds as I recall.

There was another flight in the DC-7 that started out in Fairbanks, Alaska. I remember that day because it was my birthday. We loaded up there and flew to Saint Lawrence Island, which is one of the closest U.S. land masses to Russia. The winds were especially strong that day and there was a question about whether we could make it to Nome, Alaska with enough fuel. There was the captain, the second officer (a former air America pilot), a flight engineer (he knew everything about DC-3's and DC-7's), and me. There was no fuel available on St. Lawrence Island so we had a dilemma. The crew was unsure that we could get back across the cold ocean waters. The flight engineer was so scared he was in the cargo hold blowing up a survival raft with his mouth. So here was the deal. I have an indecisive captain and second officer and I have a flight engineer telling all of us that we are all going to die.

"Captain Jack" focused on the situation. I had the captain and first officer do as precise calculations as they could as to our probability of success. Once that was done they both agreed that our chances were good. Then I went back to the flight engineer and had a discussion with him. I told him that three of us were in agreement but we needed his consent as well. I told him plan "B" would be to use the life raft if we had to. He agreed to finish blowing it up. It used up a lot of his nervous energy in the process and got him focused on what he needed to do as flight engineer.

We had three choices. Stay where we were for a day until we could get another aircraft out there with more fuel. Takeoff with no calculations or, make the calculations, have a plan "B" and proceed on to Nome. In all my years of flying I have never overruled my other pilots vote. We either agree or come up with an alternate solution that is agreeable to all.

We took off and everyone did what they were supposed to do. We made it to Nome with adequate fuel. Once again, I recognized there were choices and I was simply the "stabilizing" element that the crew needed to make a decision.

CHAPTER 37

One of our last trips in the DC-3 was a trip out of Anchorage, Alaska carrying a full load of supplies. There was a 10,000 foot mountain range to cross. When we leveled off at 12,000 feet, the left engine began to miss-fire. We had a new captain on board with a mountain to cross. I had a friend of my partner's in the jump seat. I was flying co-pilot in the right seat.

If we couldn't maintain altitude above 10,000 feet we would crash into the mountains. We were in the clouds and the mood was tense. The left engine had lost about 60% of its power but still allowed us to maintain 10,300 feet. The "pucker" factor was great for all of us. Any further descent and we would start throwing cargo out of the aircraft.

As we "collectively" held our breath, the weather improved and we cleared the mountain range. We descended and landed at the first available airport. Once again, focus and knowing the choices available made for a positive outcome.

My adventure in Alaska would soon end. It was time to go home and resume a "normal" life, whatever that meant.

CHAPTER 38

As I reflect on my first 40 years of my life I had to ask myself these questions.

1) What had been the driving force in my life and why am I not satisfied?
2) Has my need for improvement and adventure a reflection on how I feel about myself?
3) Am I so different from everyone else that I feel like an outsider in society?

I will answer the first question this way. My driving force probably resulted from my feelings of inadequacy. I was a below average student and I never felt good about myself.

I recognized soon after college that competitiveness became a win or lose scenario for me. This constant battle of the male ego to prove who's best, who's right, who's not best and who's wrong. For me, this was a serious flaw. Life was too much "positive-negative", "success-failure. I wanted to look through my own "rose" colored glasses at life, maybe we all do.

My philosophy had to make sense. Wasn't participating in life "winning"? I refused to any longer get "hung up" on the word "failure". I forced myself to try new things. Failure for many is interpreted as a desired goal coming out differently than planned.

Is that a failure or an "experience"? I transformed my competitive "win-lose" attitude into a "win-win" philosophy. Why can't our actions in our personal life and our business life be "win-win" for everybody? Isn't that what company "mission statements" are always trying to convey?

The second question about how I felt about myself I will answer this way.

After having finished my tour in the navy, I had a great deal of confidence in myself. When I joined the state patrol, people having college degrees were kind of an anomaly or rarity. College educated troopers hadn't assimilated very well. I felt the need to have to prove myself all over again. The attempts at going to graduate school, the sailboat trip to Hawaii were all a part of my way of getting noticed. I don't think I felt good about who I was. The constant moving to take new opportunities caused a lot of emotional and financial stress.

The other influence on my need for adventure was the loss of my father. Often he would share his dreams. Even when I was 26 years old, it was still fun hanging out with my parents. I think his death only fueled my desire to live a more complete, full life.

The third question was simple to answer. I was no different than anyone else. I had the same struggles, issues and desires. I had made the same decisions and had the same consequences as other people. Then the next questions comes to mind. Who am I? What is my purpose in life?, and what do I want to do when I grow up?

In the generations of my parents and before, it was not uncommon to work for one company or stay in one profession for an entire career. At age 50 or soon thereafter, one retired.

Today, most people have moved a number of times, tried a number of jobs and are still working into their seventies. I will be one of those people.

Self- discovery is a slow, painful process. It will take another 20 years for me to get a "clue" about myself. I will have gone through a divorce and my second wife will help me in my next, difficult road toward self- awareness. Who am I?; I am just a part of the universe; interconnected with everyone and everything else. What is my purpose in life?; to be a part of the human condition. What do I want to be when I grow up? I have been told that living in the "moment" is the only reality we have. There is no yesterday or tomorrow, only today, only now. Then the question becomes, how do I want to spend that moment? I guess the simplest answer is just to be aware of it and enjoy it.

The struggle now becomes, how do we go on with life with some meaningful purpose? My work has come to identify who I am. My personal life often leaves me void and without identity. Why can't we do what we enjoy in life to make a living? The next 20 years will be as challenging as the first 40. I think most of us are on the same journey, we just don't know the destination.

CHAPTER 39

Okay, enough philosophizing, as my son constantly reminds me.

What I had discovered about myself was the following. Because of my ability to focus and my calm demeanor, I looked at most situations without the usual emotional attachments. Do I get emotional about anything? Of course I do. Instead of yelling, screaming or having physical outbursts, I complained, vented or whined depending on the situation. Wherever I was, "Captain Jack" was there to provide stability, calmness and focus. My life up until now had prepared me to just be "Captain Jack".

I had to go into the ocean to discover who that was.

CHAPTER 40

If you have ever seen the movie "Groundhog Day", it best explains how I often looked at myself. I seemed stuck, repeating the same scenarios over and over again. In the movie, the character Bill Murray played was stuck repeating each day the same as before. He stayed stuck until he transformed himself to a different "state of mind".

I think for any of us that just to recognize we are "stuck" is amazing. What the reality of the concept "state of mind" is really about is simply our attitude towards the way we look at everything. Each of us has the power to decide how we want to accept our "moment" in time. We can be angry, we can blame others, or we can simply change the way we think about it. Other people are not responsible for how we feel. We simply have the choice as to how we are going to respond to any situation. Remember, when I was in the ocean by myself in a seemingly hopeless situation, I decided how I was going to think about it? Nothing else changed.

CHAPTER 41

So here I am after all these life experiences writing down some events in my life trying to better understand some of my "human" conditions.

I now better understand my ability to focus and my belief in having choices.

I now better understand my decision making process.

I don't have to remain stuck in "Ground Hog Day". None of us do. Writing this book has helped me move forward.

Each of us as individuals does make a difference. It is not somebody else's responsibility to make the decisions that work.

We all have equal importance and are all "beacons" for mankind.

In Mahatna Ghandi's own words "Be the change that you want to happen" carries a powerful message.

By writing down my thoughts and ideas, I have shared with you a part of my life, which was in reality a "moment" in all of our lives. Each of our own collection of beliefs makes us who we are. It is how we use additional information, it is how we remove our objections to each situation that along with our belief system determines our outcomes as it relates to our everyday decision making.

CHAPTER 42

We all have a lifetime of experience. We all have the same questions, many unanswered.

We all go through each day with the same preconceived ideas of what we think we need to do.

Each one of us is on a journey. The question is, can each one of us stop and enjoy that one moment, or do we keep looking past that moment, for something that is preconceived to be better? Are we looking for a "notion"?

I will paraphrase a definition of a notion as it has been explained to me. A notion is just an assumption, a belief, or an opinion. A notion is some vague idea in which a great deal of unfounded confidence is placed. A notion is the best way to avoid reality, it is a great way to see things the way you want to, and not as they are. A notion has the same power as reality. The death of a notion is reality. The death of reality is a preconceived notion. The four pillars of this most powerful notion are; Preconception, Prejudgment, Prejudice and Presumption. Reality cannot trump preconceived notions, because while reality will always show what's before you, preconceived notions always dictate what its outcome will be. When you select notions as your truth all others are rejected. A decision made on a notion, preconceived or not, is a decision void of any data based on reality.

This is what I struggle with every day!

CHAPTER 43

My book <u>Lost at Sea, Sort of,</u> is really about information gathering, focus and how each of us uses our belief systems to survive each day of our lives.

When the statement "belief systems" is mentioned, it is not uncommon to just think about religious or spiritual beliefs. It includes both spiritual and religious beliefs, but its meaning encompasses all the information we have gathered from the first moment of birth.

We have beliefs about which foods to eat. We have beliefs about sports, current events, cars, men, women, the universe and so on and so forth.

What most of us are unaware of is how we use our belief system in our daily lives.

If a belief is so strong that our first reaction to a given situation is based solely on our belief system, the outcome may be unexpected. For example, if a police officer arrests a suspect with no evidence because he "believes" he or she looks guilty, this action would have taken place merely because of a belief without any supporting evidence. If we allow ourselves to gather information first about what is happening around us, then incorporate our belief system, the outcome will be more positive.

When I was working as a State Trooper on Interstate 90 in Washington State one day, a deputy reported a suspicious vehicle traveling westbound. It contained four women and what appeared to be a large marijuana plant in the back seat of the car. I relayed the information to a fellow trooper that was in a better position than I was to make the stop. The vehicle was stopped. It contained four nuns and a bush that wasn't even close to being a marijuana plant. The initial information had been relayed solely based on a belief system with no additional evidence to support the stop. We all got a good laugh over it, but the point is made.

EPILOGUE

Choices, focus, objections and belief systems. All so subtle in our everyday American lives. Belief systems can be a wonderful thing and separate us as individuals. It is truly the substance of who we are.

It is the information we gather that will always give us the opportunity to make better choices. Consumer reports, talking to others who have had the experience of a product or an event help us in determining what products to buy or events to enjoy.

It is information that we ourselves can gather to help remove preconceived notions or objections. How many times have you heard so called friends, associates or parents remind us that we are not capable of doing anything. It is that thinking that has kept many of us from living our dreams. I am a writer if I write a book. Whether it gets published or not does not keep me from being a writer or continue to write.

It is this information combined with our belief system and the focus to carry out our desires that will result in our making the best choices that we can for ourselves.

When individuals act solely on their belief systems without additional information, their choices are often flawed and regretful.

I could have believed that when I fell in the ocean and the boat disappeared from sight I had no chance of survival and drowned.

My belief system, the information that I had, the choices that I made, the objections that I removed and the focus that ensued were the difference.

It was simply a choice and a state of mind. Or... I had no reason to believe that I wouldn't survive.